Sun Tzu's
The Art of Competing

Sun Tzu's
The Art of Competing

Scott A. Bell

Writer's Showcase
San Jose New York Lincoln Shanghai

Sun Tzu's The Art of Competing

All Rights Reserved © 2002 by Scott Allen Bell

Writer's Showcase
an imprint of iUniverse, Inc.

For information address:
iUniverse, Inc.
5220 S. 16th St., Suite 200
Lincoln, NE 68512
www.iuniverse.com

ISBN: 0-595-21488-6

Printed in the United States of America

Dedication

This book is dedicated to my wife, Karen, who many years ago supported my decision to be a salesperson.

Epigraph

"Business is War"

Japanese Motto

Contents

BACKGROUND ON SUN TZU

Sun Tzu, also referred to as Sun Wu and Sun Zi, was originally reputed to have existed and written his "Art of War" around the period of 400 BC. This has been a subject of great controversy among Chinese scholars and later even some western scholars who chose to pursue the matter. The work "The Art of War" has been placed as having been written in China during the period of the Warring States (435-221 BC). This was a period of great turmoil when each area ruler tried to outwit the other to gain control of larger areas of China. This is very akin to companies competing for market share or territory. While the timing does not matter for the purpose of this book, if the reader is interested I would suggest reading Samuel B. Griffith's translation of the Art of War which has an extensive piece on the scholarly argument of the background of the book.

Whether Sun Tzu was a real person or whether the work was written in 500 or 300 BC is relevant only to scholars. The work is still the oldest known treatise on war and still the most concise and relevant. The Japanese learned of this book during the Tang dynasty (618-906 AD.) and a French Jesuit missionary named Father Pere (J.J.M.) Amiot later learned of it and translated it into French in 1772 in Paris. This was the first introduction of this work to the west. The translation was widely circulated and favorably reviewed. It is believed by some that Napoleon read it as he was a young officer at the time and was known to be an avid reader. Translations into Russian have been found as early as 1800. An English officer did the first English translation in 1905 and a British museum curator named Lionel Giles did a later translation, which is still in print today, in 1910. This last translation is not widely respected and I recommend later ones done in English by Samuel B. Griffith, or Cheng Lin, or Tang Zicheng, or for a most interesting version in comic form–Tsai Chih Chung and Leong Weng Kam. There is also a version by James Clavell, the noted novelist of Asian sagas.

'The Art of War' has had a major effect and influence on both Chinese and Japanese military theory and practice along with all the major western powers. As Samuel Griffith so eloquently expounds on in his book, it was the source of Mao Tse-Tung's military actions along with other historic military leaders. When this book was introduced to me as a basis for creating a business competitive process, I was astounded at how appropriate it was and how well the principles worked. The book's central premise is that victory can only be consistent and predictable through the understanding and use of strategy. As he (Sun Tzu) stated' "Thus, what is of supreme importance in war is to attack the enemy's strategy". As a friend of mine translated this in business lingo, "The key to winning lies not in defeating the competitor but in defeating the competition's strategy for therein lays their vulnerability".

This version of The Art of War is intended to help both sales person and marketing person alike. It is intended to take the 3000-year-old teachings of a master in the strategy of war and translate it for use in today's competitive marketplace. Those of us who are in or have been in the front line of sales and marketing understand that it is a war out there. There battle fields to be won. There are competitors to be vanquished. All of the war analogies are real no matter how overused or trite they may sound. This book is written not from the view of a dispassionate consultant but from the passion of the battlefield. There is a lot to learn from Sun Tzu both in the planning of a marketing campaign and in the field execution of that plan by a sales person.

Introduction

The first question you may have as you stand in the bookstore reading the title of this book and then reading this introduction is "What qualifies this person to write a book on competing?" Great question! As one of my favorite authors, Scott Adams, the creator of the Dilbert business cartoon, said when posed the same question for one of his books: "I worked in a cubicle for seventeen years. Consultants and professors who haven't spent much time in a cubicle write most business books. That's like writing a firsthand account of the experience of the Donner party based on the fact that you've eaten beef jerky. Me, I've gnawed an ankle or two". Well, I've worked in sales and marketing for 25 years and I've gnawed a competitor's ankle or two.

I've been a salesperson for almost 25 years yet it is not what I started out to be. Like most high school kids who are convinced by their parents that college is the answer to success in life, I started out on a path to be a "professional". As a high school student trying to decide what kind of profession I wanted to study in college, I first asked, "What are the professions?" Many possible fields of study were given and "sales" was never mentioned. I narrowed the list to doctor, lawyer, or architect (I had done well at drafting in shop class). So my Dad, in good "fatherly" wisdom, had me meet and visit the offices of a lawyer and an architect (I ruled out doctor early because I could not imagine myself involved intimately with other people's bodily fluids).

Already the process of choosing a profession was breaking down because I had no idea the vast range of professional possibilities and neither did the high school counselors. I have often said that I wish I knew then what I know now about making a living. I would probably be an orthodontist. Of course this is somewhat influenced by my three children's'visits to one and the accompanying cost.

The lawyer talked to me about all the legal research that goes into preparing cases. He showed me the legal library and spoke of how an apprentice would spend their time. This shattered my "John Grisham" view of being a heroic lawyer. Besides, I hated the language of lawyers the minute I saw it. Quickly, I decided not to become a "party of the first part".

The architect that I visited was a partner in a small firm in my hometown. He asked if I liked sport cars (his was an old Jaguar XKE). I said yes. They showed me some home designs they were working on. They asked if I liked wearing suits. I said no. They told me I was a natural. I had my profession.

The problem was that neither visit told me the whole truth. Not all lawyers spend their life in research. Not all architects get to design homes, not wear suits, and drive around in neat old sport cars. As I so rudely found out much later, both fields also can cause you to starve. Not all lawyers or architects make a lot of money. The best advice I got was from an old architect who swam at the local YMCA where I worked part time. He had made a lot of money so I asked him how. First he laughed when I said I wanted to be an architect. Next he told me the secret was to be able to sell what you can do. He sold home plans to home magazines that resold the plans through mail order. He was doing very well. It didn't sound real "professional" and I was only 18 so I wrote him off.

What was not obvious during my visits was that not all lawyers and not all architects are professionals. We all know about "ambulance chasers" and other unscrupulous lawyers but there are also architects who "sell their seals". Once an architect passes the apprentice requirement they can take a state exam to get their seal. This allows them to be official. Most states or local municipalities require an architect's seal on all building designs and most building improvements. However, not everyone can or wants to afford paying the architect to design a deck or porch. So there are some architects who will put their seal on a drawing even though they did not create or, sometimes, even seriously look at the drawings. So I later learned that the title of "professional" had only a little to do with the degree and much more to do with the attitude toward your job. Unfortunately, I did not learn this lesson until after college.

I went to school to be an architect and after five years of hard work achieved what I thought to be the goal–the degree. I promptly went out and interviewed and received several offers from well-known firms. However, the offers were for what seemed to be slave wages, even worse than a teacher (another profession). Also, I was usually shown to the "beginner's room" which was a cavernous room full of young architects drawing doors, windows, etc. No real brainpower here. Dejected and frankly very confused, I returned to my college where a professor heard my tale and gave me one of the best pieces of advice to date–get an MBA. Not that an MBA was magic, it wasn't. What it did was open a different world to me—the world of business. His advice was that everything uses business skills to work. Architecture firms do. Law firms do. Medical practices and hospitals do. This is true especially if they are to succeed in today's world. I enjoyed getting that degree. My next revelation was more difficult to swallow and came by a more circuitous route.

I got my first job as a business manager for a non-profit organization. I got the job because I had a degree in architecture and an MBA. The organization was growing and was in the midst of a building program for a community for the handicapped. The growth of the organization was taxing their primitive business practices and the building project was not going well because no one in the organization knew how to read blueprints or manage a building project. So they were having a difficult time communicating with the architect and builder what they felt they needed. Additionally, the architect and builder were often at odds and the people who were supplying the money were caught in the middle not knowing how to sort it out. With a degree in architecture and a degree in business, I was uniquely qualified and, being young and inexperienced, I was cheap by most standards. They did not realize that what they were willing to pay me was 30% more than I could get as a starting architect. An opportunity was born and I was happy. I was managing a small building project and building a business practice for a small not-for-profit business.

I tell you this story for two reasons—first because I love telling stories, second because it leads to how I became a salesperson when I never wanted to be one. The next part of this story is the most important. While at this job I met a man who changed my career and eventually my life. His name was Bill Dailey and he was an IBM salesman. I liked him immediately. He was one of those hard working, extremely likable Irishmen who lived life on his terms and handed out advice for free. His advice to me was that I was in the wrong profession. I needed to be in sales.

I needed to be in sales? Sales a profession? I politely declined. However, if you are aware at all of some of the more endearing qualities of the Irish (I eventually married his daughter so I know), one of them is persistence (also known as stubbornness when they feel they are right). Now I had grown up in a sales and marketing family. My father had basically grown up as a salesman in the fifties and sixties, which is a great story in itself. Neither he nor I had even considered it an option for my college-educated direction. Besides, who in their right mind considered sales a profession? A job, yes, but "professional salesperson" was the punch line in an oxymoron joke. This is still true today. I have noticed that anytime I am asked for employment information on the web, the pull down menu lists "professional" and then in parenthesis are examples such as Lawyer, Doctor, Architect, etc. One such pull down even had "Artist" under professional. Sales is never on these lists. Maybe I am a little too sensitive here but I think you understand my point.

The persistence of Bill eventually won and I agreed to go in for an interview at, of all places, IBM. Specifically, I interviewed in their Office Products Division, which was better known as "OPD". These were real sales people who made up to 10 sales calls a day selling typewriters and other office equipment. Now remember I did not really want to be a salesperson but I also wasn't too sure anymore about being an architect and making a decent living. Additionally I had a beard and I was sure I would not make it through the interview process at IBM but it would get Bill off my case and allow me to date his daughter.

To make a long story a bit shorter I amazingly made it through the interview process and was offered a job on one condition–shave the beard. I asked what the financials of the offer were and, upon learning what I could make as a salesperson, I decided if celebrities could be paid to shave on TV I could do it for IBM. The money was twice what I would make as an architect and that was just the base. If I sold anything, they paid me more! I still did not believe I could sell but I figured it would take a while for them to find out.

The next step was to be sent to sales school. During the interview process I was surprised to learn they had a sales training school. Later I learned why it was nicknamed "the boot camp". I also learned you could "flunk" this school and be let go. I was sure they would discover I could not sell and send me packing. Off I went to the IBM sales boot camp.

The first thing that impressed me was the caliber of the other trainees. They were young, well educated, and very bright. I guess I thought I would meet the typical stereotype of the poorly dressed, pushy salesperson. Instead I met this group of great people. The school was a challenge and harder work than college but I did not flunk. In fact I won the class award for excellence. Most important, by the end of class I knew I had the skills and confidence to sell. This was definitely something I didn't have before I went in. I received two things besides selling skills from that experience. First, I became fascinated with sales training and the ability of good training to develop a highly skilled person from almost scratch. Second I wondered why selling was not more widely treated as a profession, especially by the academic community. You can get degrees in accounting, marketing, economics, business law, engineering, or manufacturing. These are all important to creating and running a business but without a skilled, professional sales force you quite possibly will not grow or stay in business. Why couldn't you get a degree in sales? Why were many sales people not very professional? Since most companies in the world depend on their sales force to succeed, these became very interesting questions to me.

If I was a high school student and I decided I wanted to go into sales and I went to my counselor what would they say? "Get a real job!" They might say try a degree in business but I've been to college and few recognize sales as a specialty let alone a profession. If I was to go to my college counselor and say I want to specialize in sales, what would they say after they stop chuckling about wasting my time at college? "Sorry, we do not recognize it as a profession". Yet there are more salespeople than even lawyers (save the jokes they sound better on lawyers). I have heard it said that "sales" is the number one job in the US and many other countries by the measure of the number of people who do it. Many of these salespeople even have a degree in something; some even have degrees in architecture! Sales, it seems, is an "illegitimate" profession. It's time to make it legitimate!

This book was partially inspired by that last thought. As a professional salesman, I have studied the process of selling my entire career. I own at least twenty books on selling, I have been to at least a half a dozen training courses, and I am certified and have done training in several methodologies. It has been the topic of many of my sales meetings as a sales manager. One of the most fascinating topics, especially in these times of growing competition locally and globally, is the competition. Eleven years ago a person I greatly respect introduced me to Sun Tzu's "The Art of War" because most of competing is akin to waging war. I realize that many people are tired of the war cliché in business but it is only because they have not been in business. If they had they would know that it is war out there, economic war. The weapons are products and services, pricing, and packaging. The battleground is the customer and the war is campaigned across entire markets. The prizes of this war are not merely profits but employment and economic stability for companies, cities, towns, and entire countries whose populace benefit because of the success of the winners.

I attended an excellent sales training course on competing and sales strategy, read Sun Tzu, and whole new competitive vistas opened up for me. Before I may have been a good tactician, selling my heart out but I was in danger of becoming, over time, just another Willie Loman. Now, thanks to my experience, I am also a strategist, able to adapt to different terrain and new or changing enemies. Sun Tzu said: "War is a matter of vital importance to the state; the province of life or death; the road to survival or ruin. It is mandatory that it be thoroughly studied". These are the opening words to Sun Tzu's book. As you will see, it easily translates to "Competing is a matter of vital importance to the company; the province of corporate life or death; the road to corporate survival or ruin. It is mandatory that it be thoroughly studied".

Over the years I found that most sales and executive management had trouble translating the words the words of Sun Tzu into something useful for everyday selling and marketing. I had this epiphany on a flight back from China after conducting a sales training course there and decided to translate each verse of Sun Tzu's book into sales and marketing language. The way I have organized this book is very close to most translations. It is organized into chapters addressing certain topics of war. Each chapter is then a set of proverbs or wisdoms. Where I felt it would add clarity, I have expounded on certain of these sayings and how they apply in selling or marketing.

This book is my attempt to loosely translate a 300 BC Chinese expert on waging war into something useful for waging war on the competition. Sun Tzu's book is the oldest treatise on strategy and waging war and has helped many famous generals be victorious. Interestingly enough, it is also required reading for many business people in Japan.

The format I have taken is to literally translate what supposedly Sun Tzu said into the language of sales and marketing. Where I thought it would help, I have added my own notes to further explain a saying or piece of his wisdom. I hope this version helps you.

Chapter 1

Estimates Or An Appreciation of the Situation

Every sales and marketing person needs to develop the skill of surveying the strengths and weaknesses of their own company, the product or services they are going to sell, the competition, their market, their territory, and their prospects in order to determine whether or not they can succeed. Too often in sales we develop a "quote and hope" mentality. I once asked a sales person who worked for me "Which is the better salesperson? One who sells two million dollars a year after chasing five million dollars worth of prospects or one who sells two million dollars a year after chasing ten million dollars worth of prospects?" He answered that it did not matter since they both closed a million dollars. Being able to understand the correct

1

answer to that question is the beginning of becoming more strategic in your behavior.

Good managers and sales people will understand that there is a big difference between the two salespeople. The one who had to chase ten million dollars worth of prospects in order to close two million dollars worth of sales used a lot more resources to close the same business. This sales person was much less efficient. The cost of sales was much higher. The "close rates" were 40% and 20% respectively. The resources were not available for either other sales people to close business or for the original sales person to close more business. That sales person was obviously more tactical, less strategic. The goal is to be both effective (defined as having a high close rate) and efficient (defined as utilizing your resources to their best advantage).

Most sale people and sales management simply blunder into a territory assuming the simplest of criteria to determine who to sell to—"Is the customer alive and have a pulse?" They then proceed to call on anyone, eating up resources and time instead of trying to determine the best places to fight. Where can I compete effectively? Where can I really win? As important, where will I most likely loose? The critical question to a more strategic person is, "How can I dominate my territory and how long will it reasonably take?" This type of reasoning will cause a reasonably intelligent person to want to know and assess their territory, regardless of how that is defined, in a different way. The analogy used in this book is of the general who, before attacking, wants to understand the lay of the land they want to conquer and the positioning of the competition. This kind of person will want to think out further than the next quota period or quarter. You would begin to not just go after the "low hanging fruit" or easier sales but rather to be sure these sales will insure long-term success.

You begin to look for those accounts that hold the most influence in your territory, the so-called "head dominos". In the child's game of lining up dominos to fall in some type of pattern, the child knows that the key is to understand how to line them up and then pick the "head domino" or the domino that will set off the chain of desired events. As a sales or marketing person, find the account that is the "head domino" or most influential in your territory or market. Close this account and each sale gets easier. Your product or service becomes known as the de facto decision. Invest your company resources and time wisely. Assess your sales or marketing situation before you proceed unwisely. This is the beginning of Sun Tzu's wisdom.

Sun Tzu would of said:

1. The ability to successfully sell against the competition is a matter of vital importance to the company, the province of profit or loss, the road to survival or ruin. It is mandatory that it be thoroughly studied.
Note:

Most companies study their competition so this idea is not necessarily new. However, I have observed two things. First, many companies use this information strictly in their marketing departments and do not analyze and communicate vital competitive information to the sales force. This cripples the sales force in respect to being able to strategize in the field. What usually translates into the field is a simple list of competitive "knockoffs" that they are supposed to use in their selling. This is very tactical and usually not very professional. This is not only very tactical but can be very dangerous. This relegates the selling to feature/function rather than true competitive selling. It is hard to keep everyone up to date on the latest things the competition cannot do well or at all. This sets up the sales people to relay potentially bad information thus ruining their credibility with the customer when the competition points out the inaccuracy of the information.

As you will read later, it is much better to attack the competitor's strategy rather than their functionality. In the long run this is far safer and can be far more effective. Also, if done well, it is very hard for the competitor to deal with in the field. Second, everyone in the company needs to be competitively aware, not just the sales and marketing groups. Sales needs to know how the competition sells and what they count on to win. Marketing needs to know what markets they are attacking and how they are positioning themselves. Finance needs to know how the competition is allocating financial resources and how they are building their pricing models. Human Resources needs to understand what type of people the competition recruits and what kind of training they receive, and so on. Every department should have some level of competitive awareness. Every company, large or small, should have someone who has the responsibility of analyzing all incoming competitive data and making key recommendations for action against them, whether in sales or in marketing programs. This gathering and analysis of competitive information cannot be emphasized enough. It should not be relegated to some minor staff person but should be done by some of the brightest people in the company, people who have the intellectual ability to see patterns and discern future behavior.

2. Therefore, appraise your ability to successfully compete as a business, as a manager, or as a sales person in terms of the five fundamental factors.

3. The first of the five fundamental factors is moral cause; the second, market conditions; the third, the customer's environment; the fourth, management; and the fifth, discipline.

4. By moral cause I mean the manner in which you manage yourself, you manage others; others manage you, and the manner in which your company is managed. Moral cause aides the employees and management to share a common belief or cause.
Note:
   This is a very important factor. People love to buy things from people who love what they sell. People love to work for companies that have a distinct and well-understood vision or mission. These types of "moral cause" can be contagious. Do you understand what your company's mission is and do you strongly believe in it? Does your company have a mission or vision that is strongly believed and acted out by all management? Employees who

are guided and believe in a moral cause will then follow management through good times and bad, sometimes even at the expense of their careers if they believe in the product, service, or vision of the company.

However, be very careful! While it is not the intent of this book to go in depth on corporate vision or mission statements, they can lead to trouble. It is only when they go beyond being company hype and become the stated passionate beliefs of management and are acted out by management that these words become "moral cause" as mentioned by Sun Tzu. Management who has this moral cause and acts it out are often great leaders.

Having this moral cause among the employees, especially the sales and marketing people, can be a big competitive advantage. Not having this can be a competitive disadvantage. If you analyze some of the great sales forces in history, I believe you will find that one common factor is that they all believed they were special. Their training and culture instilled in them a definite purpose. Sometimes it almost verged on fanaticism. Study history and see what a small army of well-trained, well lead fanatics can do. This is no different in competing.

Finally, listen carefully when the employees start talking about not knowing what the mission, or vision is or if they badmouth what they are selling or their management. This is a sure indication of the lack of a moral cause. When this happens, it is often because executive management is no more than a group of "empty suits".

5. By market conditions I mean the interaction of the forces of the market that causes it to be receptive to new products or services or cling to old ones. It is also the way the forces interact to favor you or favor your competition. It is important that you and your company be aware of these forces so as to understand when the climate and timing are right for competition and when it is right for you.
Note:
We've all heard the phrase, "It was ahead of its time". Timing can sometimes be everything. Time is never neutral. Time is either working for you

or against you. Check to see whose time it is. I once knew two companies who thought up two new products aimed at the same market at the same time. One involved slow cooking food so a working family would have a delicious cooked meal by the time they got home. The other company came up with an idea for fast cooking meals so the same working family could come home and throw a meal in and have it ready in minutes; the "Slow-Cook Oven" and the microwave. Ever heard of the "Slow-Cook" Oven? Probably not. It provided a far superior tasting and nutritious meal but speed was the name of the game. Wrong time. Wrong market conditions. A great product failed.

As everyone in marketing knows, markets are littered with great, badly timed, poorly marketed, poorly sold products. All of these factors must be taken into account. Sun Tzu writes many times about knowing all the factors before going to war or in our case, competing.

6. By customer environment I mean the competitive arena, the customer "ground" that you are competing for and whether it is easy to compete for the customer's business or difficult, whether they are open to your product or service or more closed depending on the "nearness" of your solution to solving the customer's real problem or adding real identifiable value to the customer as compared to the competition and the chances of gaining profitable market share or going bankrupt.
Note:

This understanding of the "customer ground" is also a very important factor. While I will talk a lot about the competitor, we also need to keep our eye on the customer and our markets. This is especially true in consideration of our competitive position relative to our ability to add value to that customer. The two factors here are the closeness of fit of our products and services to the issues the customer is dealing with and the receptiveness of the market or customer to new solutions. Can you really add value to the customer? Can you really solve a problem or improve a condition? How much better are you at adding value than the competition? Is this an open market or a relatively closed one?

7. By management I mean the sales and marketing executives' qualities of wisdom, sincerity, humanity, courage, and strictness or adherence to discipline.

Note:

These qualities cannot be slighted. Too many managers manage but can't lead. The standing joke in sales is that we promote our best sales people to management where they do what they did best, sell instead of manage or lead. Many books have been written on this subject and many training courses are given yet it is still true that many companies lack great leaders or even adequate leaders. The Dilbert cartoon is not popular because it is clever but because it rings all too true.

Again, it is not within the scope of this book to talk in depth about leadership. However, it is an important factor in being able to compete effectively. I also believe that Sun Tzu gives a strong yet simple insight into leadership. As he states it is made up of the qualities of wisdom (applied knowledge and intelligence), sincerity (you believe what you say and do), humanity (you really care about people), courage (you have stated beliefs and the guts to act on them), and discipline (you are process driven).

These qualities of wisdom, sincerity, humanity, courage, and discipline are the trademarks of leaders. Take a hard look at your management teams, especially in sales and marketing. Are these intelligent people or are they rather clueless? Do they use their intelligence to gain insight into the customers and competitors or do they just sell and run? Are they sincere people or are they shallow? Do they have the guts to make difficult decisions or stand up to competition? Are they disciplined?

8. By discipline I mean your company's organization (how well organized is it to do business?), adherence to stated policies and processes, the fairness of the system of reward and punishment, assignment of appropriate

territories to field managers, regulation of resources, and the supply of the principle items used by a sales force.

Note:

It would be easy to overlook this factor, discipline. It is my observation that discipline is one of the most overlooked traits in a company. Yet in war, we would immediately recognize that a well-disciplined army would more likely defeat an undisciplined one. In business, I rarely hear of sales forces or even whole companies referred to as disciplined or undisciplined. It is my unscientific observations that as more "baby boomers" reach management positions; they manage like they raise children—undisciplined. Of course we also have a fairly litigious society that scares all managers regarding taking disciplinary actions.

I remember two very revealing conversations in my management career. The first was with a CEO who made an off-hand remark on how difficult it was to implement new or different programs in his company. I remarked back that it was because the whole company culture knew that it was rare to get fired or disciplined for not implementing any new policy. A young brash new manager then made the comment that if you fired the first person to disobey, the other managers would be lined up outside the CEO's office with ideas of how to implement the new policy.

The second conversation was regarding a work dress policy. A management team I was part of had decided that the dress policy might have become outdated. Great time was spent in discussion of a new policy that every executive could agree to. It was written up and published to the employees. It was a new "business casual" dress policy. It strictly prohibited things such as blue jeans and sandals. Within a week, a few people began wearing sandals and jeans. Not one manager said anything. As a result, within a year, we saw blue jeans, tennis shoes, bib-overalls, etc. all of which had been spelled out as prohibited. No one said a word. The managers grumbled about the lack of adherence but not one took any action. This lack of discipline becomes infectious. This is what Sun Tzu is speaking of. It takes managers/leaders with conviction and courage to invoke discipline in a group whether it is an army or a workforce. Without discipline, there will eventually be anarchy or chaos. With discipline plans are carried out policies are adhered to, strategies are executed, battles are won.

9. There is no sales or marketing executive who has not heard of these five factors. Those who master them win against competition; those who do not are defeated by competition.

10. Look into all aspects, study the facts and then make seven calculations.

11. Which company has a moral cause as evidenced by a strong common belief among employees in a mission, vision and what they sell that can or has pulled all the employees together with management in a concentrated effort? A company that has this "moral cause" is like an impassioned army on the move. This type of army can be impossible to stop.
Note:

The key is to get beyond the mission as just a slogan, "Quality is job one". Not that Ford's statement was a mere slogan. I am sure everyone inside Ford took that as a personal mission. If so, it was just what Sun Tzu was talking about when he wrote about having "a moral cause". How do you do this? I am not a psychologist but in the better companies I worked for, these missions were communicated all the way down an organization. You could tell that all management was on board. You did not see the rolling of the eyes every time the mission was mentioned. People believed in it and were rewarded for carrying it forward. This type of commitment to a moral cause can cause people to pull together and work hard. In today's cynical workplace, this can be very difficult. However, if you can pull it off, it can be powerful as a sales tool.

12. Which company has better management especially at the executive level?
Note:

Better as described as intelligent, having not only a stated set of personal values that are cohesive with the company values but values that are acted out by each manager. These leaders have the courage to act out what they say they believe in and "stick to their guns". They state what they believe in along with the ability to empathize with their employees and relate to them not only on a business level but a personal level, and, finally, management that can exercise discipline in their own actions and in the management of others so policies are followed. Plans are implemented. Their values are driving their actions.

13. Which company does the market conditions favor and which company has the more robust solution capability?
Note:
I spend very little time in this book on the customer. Again, many very good books exist that talk about customer value and how to identify and deliver it. I believe in customer value but the purpose of this book was to concentrate on defeating the competition. That said, one of Sun Tzu's key success principles is determining if your solutions are closer to what the customer and market want than your competitors.

14. Which company's employees are more apt to execute the company's strategy and orders without faltering?

15. Which company's employees are confident of their purpose and do not quiver at competition?

16. Who has the better-trained management and employees?

17. Who has the more enlightened system of rewards and punishments?

18. From the answers to these questions the outcome of the competitive war can be predicted.

19. And remember, competing in the marketplace is full of deceptions. The more you can deceive the competition the better. The more you can know your competition and avoid being deceived the better.

20. Learn to recognize your competitors' weaknesses and exploit them. Learn to create weakness in your competitor by creating anger so they will overreact, or by creating internal strife in your competitor so you can crush them, or attacking them in the marketplace when they are unprepared. Note:

Here we can come to a dilemma in many cultures. Is it ethical to exploit a competitor's weaknesses? As was stated in the beginning, learning to compete effectively is a vital matter to a company. It is the matter of survival, growth, or bankruptcy. We can compete on a professional but tough level. How to do this will be different in each company's culture. Sun Tzu is simply stating the obvious; if you do not do this, your competitor will and you will lose.

21. Be vigilant of your competitor's strengths and when they are alert. Be willing to back off temporarily when they are strong so they will become complacent and then attack them by surprise.

22. Surprise is the secret of success but always be flexible in strategy. Competition and competing are very unpredictable.

23. Before you decide to enter a marketplace or a customer's environment against your competitors, weigh the strengths and weaknesses of both your company and the competition.

24. If your company is in an advantageous position, the chance of gaining dominant market share will be good, if your company is not in an advantageous position, the chance of victory will not be good.

25. Careful planning will lead to victory. Poor planning will lead to defeat. The worst is to have no planning at all! Confusion is an enemy both of yourself and of your company. It is better to be wrong than to be confused. Confusion undermines moral cause.

26. After considering all these things, we can predict victory or defeat in competing.

Summary

This chapter is the opening chapter in Sun Tzu's "The Art of War". It is the foundation for all that follows. All of this is a lot to think about although some of it is common sense. However, how many of us have worked for or are working for companies where there is a lack of "benevolent" discipline? Where are the courageous managers who can make decisions and take action rather than try to make everyone happy? Even worse, why are some managers so inept and jerks to everyone around him or her? How many of us in our selling or marketing believe we have a mission to help our customers be more competitive or handle their customers in a better way? As I call on companies or work for companies it is obvious that most survive in spite of themselves. Today's world is incredibly competitive and there is no sign of it slowing down. This is true for both the marketing teams and sales teams.

Look at some of the great sales forces in history and you could have predicted they'd be great if you measured them on the factors Sun Tzu points out in this chapter. Like great armies, they were disciplined, well led, and singular in their purpose and in a sense of mission. They were not confused. As one marketing friend of mine has said, "Their hearts, heads, and mouths were in unison". They were armies on the move and they were hard to stop. Some are no longer with us. They fell prey to weakened management or a falling of moral cause. They forgot or may have never understood what made them great. Some are still here and almost strike fear into the heart of any competitive salesperson that runs into them in an account. We know who they are. They dominate markets and accounts.

As Sun Tzu opens his book he warns that in order to compete, the entire company must realize that learning to compete well is of vital importance. It should be thoroughly studied. This is the tome for the rest of his book. What should we be studying? What skills should we be good at in order to compete effectively? Is our management ready to compete?

Chapter 2

Engaging the Competition

It amazes me how many sales people or managers believe themselves to be competitive and yet know little strategically (and sometimes even tactically) about the competition. Could you recognize the competition if they were in the same restaurant as yourself? Do you understand their strategy or approach to the market? What kind of customers do they prefer? How do they enter a prospective account? What tactics do they rely upon to win? How do they try to recover from a loss? In today's competitive marketplaces, you have to not only work to add value to the customer and win but you must work to defeat the competition, or you will not survive. Every competitor is selling "value". To win, sometimes you must not only sell value to the customer but you must help the competition loose.

As Sun Tzu said in his opening to his book on war, learning to engage the competition is vital to success and therefore should be thoroughly studied. Every great athlete or coach knows this and the best spend many hours looking at movies of the competition or studying the competition until they feel they know them. The great generals in history knew this and many books were written on the exploits. Every company will give this lip service but few actually act on it. The best sales force I was ever a part of had an entire department, staffed by both marketing and former sales people, who studied and analyzed every competitor. They knew what markets they were targeting. They knew what the competitive sales forces were counting on to win. They knew how the competition was positioning in those markets. They knew how the competitive sales people were being trained to sell and compete. They knew what tactics the competitors were counting on to prevent a loss. When they engaged the competition, they won far more than they lost because they were prepared to defeat the competition. They understood that business is war.

So I ask you, "Do you really understand your competition?" "Can you accurately anticipate every move of your competition?" "Do you know how they will react to your moves in the marketplace or in a selling situation?" If the answer to these questions is no, then you are not ready to engage the competition. It is that simple.

Sun Tzu kind of said:
1. Generally, you have to have the resources to support a sales or marketing campaign before engaging the competition. These resources will take many forms: Advertising budgets, support material for the field, training, travel expense budgets, the proper compensation plans that support the type and length of sales efforts, and determination of any other direct or indirect expenses. Only after all expenses are accounted for is the company ready to compete.

Note:

Some companies are good at planning a campaign, some are not. Many of the campaigns I have been involved in were done at the last minute and not well thought out. If they were driven from marketing, they tended to be flashy but did not have the materials or training needed to support them or did not take into account the realities of possible impact on current sales efforts. If they were driven from sales, they worked tactically but did not necessarily work into the greater good of the company and usually ended up looking like contests. The key is to involve marketing, field sales, and other support organizations to make sure all areas are covered. It is better to take your time and make sure the campaign is well thought out and everything will be ready than to go off half-cocked and disrupt the sales process and even possibly confuse the customers.

2. Success or victory is the main objective in competing. If success is delayed or prolonged, employee enthusiasm and morale will be lessened. When you attack a competitor's strong hold, your strength will be greatly tested. Be careful!
Note:

This is an important point. The big competitor's accounts are always tempting, especially to a competitive sales person. Beware! These accounts can be won but it often takes a siege mentality in the management ranks. By siege mentality I mean if it is truly a competitive stronghold, it will take much longer to penetrate. It takes time to build relationships and uncover areas you may be able to uniquely fill. If, as management, you are pressuring the sales person to close quick or if your compensation does not take a longer sales cycle into the account, the sales people will, rightfully, want to move on to easier battles. Competitive strongholds can be taken away but it takes a lot of effort and resources and a resolve by management. If, as management, you do not have the patience and understanding of what it will take, stay away from competitive strongholds. Wait them out until your market position changes and the effort will not be so big.

3. A long sales or marketing campaign can also deplete the company's finances. You should have a way of evaluating the cost of winning a sale and measure it against the reward to determine if the resources exist to win and if it is worth winning.
Note:

I find this SunTzu-ism interesting. It seems to me to be rare to find a company who has the information or discipline to do a quick evaluation of the cost and return for winning a sale. This is especially true of very large sales. I have seen companies almost break themselves financially to win a big account, hoping to make it back in volume. The sales joke, "I lose money on every sales but I will make it up in volume" is a warning. Some companies do this type of measurement but many do not. Sometimes it is better to walk away if the cost is too high for the return but that is a very difficult decision. The best practices I have seen is when, for large sales, there is some type of management reviews of the cost vs. return along with the market impact.

4. When your resources are low or are all engaged is the right moment for a competitor to attack your accounts or territory. Even a good tactician cannot do anything to help in such a situation.
Note:

It is a classic technique in warfare to create a situation whereas the enemy's front line troops get too far ahead of their supplies and then attack. Be careful to not get too far ahead of your resources. I have seen this especially with companies who have some type of service component to their sale. If they sell too much and are not mindful of their service capacity, they begin to not be able to deliver and customers become very unhappy. A wise competitor will take advantage of this to undermine your sales.

5. Therefore, always compete to win quickly.

6. Those who do not understand the danger of engaging the competition, do not understand the usefulness of engaging the competition. There can be great losses and there can be great gains. If you truly understood the danger, you would be vigilant in studying the competition. Learn to think like the competition in order to out-think them. Consider competing not as a game of checkers that is mostly tactical but as a game of chess where you must be able to think ahead further than the competitor in order to win.

7. A good salesperson or manager will plan well for a given competitive engagement and will not need to continually go back to the company for more people or resources in order to win. This is because the manager knows the competition and knows the customer and therefore can better estimate what it should take to win. To not be able to do this is dangerous and can be a cause for failure.

8. A good salesperson or manager learns to augment his resources from within the customer or within the area of the competition because these local resources are easier and cheaper to supply. Whenever possible help the competition to deplete their resources. The "general" knows that it is not only their responsibility to plan to win but to plan for the competition to fail.

9. If you are a manager or lead a team effort, motivate your people against the competition. Provoke them to want to beat the competition. They must never stop thinking about the competition and how to defeat them. This must be constantly in their minds.

10. Entice your people with attractive rewards to destroy the competition's resources or to cause the competition to use their resources foolishly.

11. Learn to use the competition's resources to your advantage.

12. Therefore compete to win quickly, never prolong a competitive engagement.

13. A good marketing or sales executive has the fate of his employees, the destiny of his company in his hands.

14. Those executives experienced in engaging the competition know they must strengthen the field sales force while engaged in competition, turning the competition's strength to your own advantage. Be wary of protracted competitive engagements and always compete to win quickly. A good executive ensures the survival of his company.

Summary

In today's markets, it is no longer good enough to just concentrate on supplying good value to the customer. Everyone has this as a goal. While this is important and should be the first priority, you must also be able to out-think the competition. Everyone is trying to focus on supplying value to the customer. You must be able to project yourself into the future–predict what the competition is going to do before they do it. As was stated, this concept is a little like learning how to play chess. The great ones can out-think their opponents. They can recognize a strategy and predict future moves. They then can set up a strategy to defeat the opponent. You begin to do this by knowing the competition better than they know themselves. Be able to think many moves ahead of the competition. Anticipate competitive counter moves to your strategies and have tactics to protect you sales plan against these competitive moves. With this knowledge, you can begin to defeat the competition.

As I stated, this is so important that it should not be done lightly. The good news is that there is a lot of competitive information just lying around waiting to be gathered and analyzed. What you are looking for is more than just data. You should look for patterns of behavior. Marketing should be analyzing advertising campaigns for more than the obvious messages. What are the implications of what is being said? How is this played out in their brochures, trade show presence, and marketing campaigns? What markets are they targeting? How are they entering into accounts or markets? What are they counting on to win? How are they positioning? Two things should be a part of every executive and sales meeting; the customers and the competition.

Chapter 3

Strategy

One of the key differences between great sales people or great management and poor ones is their ability to act strategically as well as tactically. Being able to make sales calls, do presentations, perform demonstrations, listen effectively, ask good questions, and overcome objections are the basic tactics of selling. But knowing when to use certain tactics, knowing when the competition is going to use their tactics and how to create situations so that the competitor's tactics will fail without them knowing is the arena of the strategist. It is the difference between playing checkers and chess. You need to see moves ahead and plan for them. It's about out-thinking the competition.

Strategy is about having a clear direction. You do not necessarily have to be right but you do have to set a direction. If it is wrong, it should become apparent quickly and you can make adjustments. The worst is to have no clear direction, to be confused. Confusion is the enemy of the strategist.

The analogy is to be that general who, looking over the battlefield, sees the high spots and the low. They see where the competition is camped. They understand how the enemy will begin and carry out the battle. They understand what the opponent counts on to win. They create a strategy that will not only win but also help the competition lose. The strategist delights in helping the competition lose.

Sun Tzu might have meant:
1. Generally, in competing, it is better to win by having the competition simply lose than to destroy them completely. Nobody likes a bully and the passion of retribution can come back to haunt you.

2. To win a hundred victories in a hundred competitive engagements is not the height of skill. To subdue the competition without having to actually compete is the height of competitive skill.
Note:
This is an interesting concept. To develop it further, it means to set up situations whereas the competition has lost before the battle has actually begun. As a marketing person, what can I do to condition the market place uniquely in my favor without tipping my hand? As a sales person, what can I do to condition my territory or prospects so that the competition has lost before they even enter the account? This is not easy. This takes a lot of thinking and competitive knowledge. This has been done.

3. Thus, what is of supreme importance in engaging the competition is to attack the competition's strategy. The key to victory lies not in defeating the competitor but in defeating the competitor's strategy for therein lays their vulnerability. If you can determine your competitor's strategy, you understand what they are going to do before they actually do it. This

insight into the future allows you to plan on how to defeat the competition. You can lay plans so that when the competition tries to execute their strategy, it fails.

Note:

This is so important a concept that I must make note of it. Most marketing and sales campaigns I have observed or taken part of are tactical battles. It is my demonstration against theirs. It is my presentation against theirs. It is my feature list against theirs. What these campaigns are not usually about is strategy. One of the cores to Sun Tzu's teachings is this concept. This is what has made his treatise on war so popular with the great generals in history. If you can understand your competitor's strategy, you can win. This is because you will know what they are going to do before they actually do it! This is the essence of building a competitive advantage. This gives you, as Sun Tzu kind of states, insight into the future.

4. Next best is to disrupt the competitor's alliances, their partners, and suppliers, all who help them to be competitive.

5. Next best, when you can, is to simply overwhelm them with your superiority; superiority in product, in service, in knowledge, in relationship with the customer, superiority in your skills and organization. It is hard to defeat a clearly superior sales force and company. Remember the five fundamental factors for victory: moral cause, market conditions, customer environment, management, and discipline.

6. The worst policy is to attack the competitor's strong holds.

7. It takes a long time to build up the necessary resources and superiority to hope to be able to dislodge an entrenched competitor.

8. A manager who takes on the competition without proper planning or without the proper resources will waste valuable resources and will most

likely lose. This is a doubly wasted effort of time and resources without likelihood of success.

9. Thus, those most skilled in engaging the competition can beat the competition without competing, dislodge the entrenched competitor without attacking the competitor's installed base, win against competition quickly without prolonged competitive engagements.

10. Learn to engage the competition in many ways such as with strategy, economics, politics, and tactics in the field of competition.

11. Do this and you will win convincingly without wearing out your own people in the process. This is a good competitive plan.

12. There are different plans for different competitive engagements depending on the circumstances.
Note:
The next set of Sun Tzu sayings are the essence of strategy. These define what are the types of strategy. Pay close attention here.

13. When you are clearly superior such as in technology, in size, in market share, and in capability, simply surround the competition and cause them to lose. This is a direct strategy and it depends on size, surprise and speed.

14. When you are clearly superior in capability but at parity in size or market share, attack them on as many fronts as possible to confuse and harass them. This is also a direct strategy and depends on size, surprise, and speed.

15. If you are superior but the circumstances do not favor you, you must change the rules of engagement. This is a more indirect strategy and depends on you having some superiority that is simply not yet clear in the customer or market's eye. In this circumstance you need to establish new rules of competition more favorable to you. Look to those who influence

your customer or market to help you. Cause them to see the superiority of your capability.

16. Another strategy if you are not clearly superior in the circumstance is to divide the competitive arena so you may be superior for a part of the business or market. This new arena can become a stronghold for you to grow from in order to conquer the competition. This is best known a "niche" selling or marketing.

17. Finally, if you are weaker and cannot maneuver the circumstances to your advantage, you must be capable of withdrawing from a competitor's initial onrush until you can determine a weak spot in the situation for the competitor. You must find ways to slow the process down or delay it until either you are stronger or the competition weakens.

18. And if in all respects you are unequal, be capable of eluding the competition. For a small company that is weak is but booty for one more powerful.

19. When your company is stronger in some or all respects than the competition: surround, attack, and divide the competition. When the company is weaker, it must compete defensively under able leadership. Otherwise, it faces the risk of defeat and destruction.

20. Executives are like the pillars of the company. If they are skillful in competing, the company will be strong. If they are not good competitors, the company will be weak.

21. A leader can bring misfortune to sales in three ways.
Note:
   This next set of Sun Tzu-isms are directed at the executives of the company. They may seem harsh but my experience has seen them to be true. If you want to lead a great sales or marketing team you should take these to heart. Do not let your ego get in the way.

22. One: He orders the sales force to compete or not to compete at the wrong times. This means interfering with the sales force management. This could be termed "hobbling the sales force".

23. Two: He treats sales matters without knowledge or consideration of how it can cause disorder in the sales force.

24. Three: He takes on the role of sales executive without understanding the strategy of competing.

25. If one ignorant of sales matters is sent to participate in the administration of the sales force, then in every decision there will be disagreement and mutual frustration and the entire sales force will be hamstrung. In this situation there is usually high employee turnover. This provides an opening for the competition to gain on you in the market.

26. If the sales force is confused and suspicious, the competition will take advantage of this to win. This is what is meant by the saying "A confused army leads to another's victory".

27. There are five winning axioms.

28. He who knows when to compete and when not to compete will be victorious overall. This means that you know yourself and the competition and understand under what conditions you can win or lose. Your decisions will be more intelligent and you will win more often because you can choose your engagements more wisely.
Note:
   It is interesting that in this 3000-year-old treatise on war we find one of our most well known sayings; choose your battles wisely. This is one of the key problems with today's sales forces. We, as sales and sales management people, believe any engagement is a proper engagement. We throw our resources at any opportunity that presents itself. This is a question of both

being more strategic and being more disciplined. I have lead and taught many sales people in my career all over the world and this is a universal truth. We all understand this in principle. Not all sales are good sales. Not all sales can be won, for a variety of reasons. If you believe the opposite, this book is not for you.

29. He who understands how to use both large and small sales forces will be successful. Any size can be an advantage if you know and understand how to use it.

30. The company whose employees are united in purpose will be successful. It is hard to stop an army with a sense of purpose.
Note:
   This was what was talked about earlier as "moral cause:.

31. He who is patient and waits for the competition to be unprepared will win.

32. Put capable field managers in command of sales without the constant interference of the executives.
Note:
   I cannot pass this one by. How many executives, who have never been in the field and never sold believe they are the best sales people and should interfere with the sales or marketing team? If, as an executive, you feel you are so good, spend at least a month going on sales calls.

33. These are the five essentials of success against competition.

34. Therefore Sun Tzu says: "Know the competition and know yourself; in a hundred competitive engagements you will never be in peril."
Note:
   This is probably one of Sun Tzu's most quoted passages. It is the essence of his book on winning at war. How many company executives are not

willing to honestly appraise their own company, products, services, and people? How many companies spend the time necessary to know the competition as well as the competition knows them selves or better? Too many executives think it is their job to pound their chests and roar, "We are the best!" This is fine for outward facing marketing material but someone had better be trying to be sure they understand the truth. Know yourself and then figure out how to use what you are to your advantage. Know the competition and then figure out how to defeat them.

35. When you are not well informed of the ways, capabilities, and plans of your competition but are very aware of your own, your chances of winning or losing in any given engagement are equal.

36. If you are ignorant of the competition and not honest about your own company's strengths and weaknesses, you are certain to be in peril of losing every time you face competition.

Summary

It is important for the sales and marketing managers to truly understand the difference between strategy and tactics. Most sales forces compete with no other strategy than "to win". These people have no insight into the future. They do not understand the competition. They do not really have a clear direction. When they win, they claim great victories even though they cannot usually explain how they won. When they lose, it is always the fault of something else—the product or service, the customer, the weather, sunspots. They do not take ownership of setting the strategy to win, to defeat the competition. These people do not make up a great sales force. They are not professionals. They are easily confused.

I have been in many "planning" meetings where too much time was spent arguing about what a strategy is. Sun Tzu gives us a simple view into strategy. There are four classes of strategy. First there is the direct strategy. This is the strategy of superiority. Next there is the more indirect strategy or the strategy of change. Then there is the niche strategy or the strategy of winning a piece. Finally, there is the strategy of withdrawal in order to survive to fight another time when you are stronger or the competition is weaker.

The key is to have a strategy. That strategy should be in context of our position with the customer and the competitive position. The key is to have a clear direction. That is the purpose of a strategy. It does not have to be right but it must be clear. If it is wrong but clear it will be obvious very quickly and can be corrected. If it is not clear, it will confuse your sales effort. Confusion is the enemy. Do not be afraid to make a mistake. Be afraid of being confused.

Additionally, you must honestly assess yourself and the competition. If you can admit your strengths and weaknesses and understand those of your competition, you can begin to understand what strategy will work. The path to wining will be clear. It is then just a question of execution.

Chapter 4

The Power of Defense

Everyone in sports knows that to consistently win, to be the best, you not only have to be good at the offense; you must be good at the defense. It's great to be good at scoring or in the case of selling to be great at closing. However, in order to score you have to have the ball. Sometimes in order to score you have to be able to get the ball away from the competition. When I was a sales person, someone once told me to remember that the closer you are to winning, the closer you are to losing. Never take you sights off the competition. How many times have I heard tales of woe from sales people who thought they were going to win but at the last minute the competition lowered the price or offered some last minute feature or promise and, before the sale person could react, the competitor closed the business. You must be good at not only taking the initiative away from the competition but also anticipating their defensive moves so as to protect your offensive plan.

Sun Tzu almost said:
1. Great leaders of the past first spent time making their position invincible against competition and then kept watch on the competition to spot areas of vulnerability.
Note:
I call this "bulletproofing" you sales plans. An interesting exercise is to take a given account plan and let an independent group of sales people tear it apart. One place I worked called this a "red team, blue team" exercise. One team was the original sales team, the other a different one. The idea was not just to find holes but also to figure out tactics to fill the holes. This leads to invincibility. You may not have time to do this on every account but it should be required on all strategic accounts. Do you understand how the competition will attack you? Do you understand how they will react to what you do? Have you put in place tactics to prevent their plan from working? This may sound trite but take some time to read about some of the great generals and wars in history and you will see that most often this is exactly the way they thought. Then again, most of them were students of Sun Tzu.

2. Invincibility depends on how and what you do to prepare yourself; the competition's vulnerability on what they do not do to prepare themselves.

3. It follows that those skilled in engaging the competition can secure themselves against defeat but we cannot be sure that the competition will create opportunities for our success.

4. Therefore it could be said: One may know how to defeat the competition, but no one can be sure of being able to defeat the competition.

5. Those who are not positive of being able to defeat the competition should be on the defensive; those who are sure they can defeat the competition should be on the offensive.

6. A company defends when they do not have clear superiority; a company directly takes on the competition when it is clearly superior.

7. Those companies and managers expert in defense against competitors consider it fundamental to make it impossible for the competition to know where to take them on. These people who are good at defense rely on any number of ways to conceal their marketing positions or strategies. Those people who are expert in directly taking on the competition consider it fundamental to make it impossible for the competition to know where they prepare to attack, which markets or accounts. When these people do attack they do so like a lighting bolt with great swiftness, purpose, and surprise. This takes great preparation before attacking.

8. For a manager to be able to predict a victory over the competition which anyone in the company could have predicted is not the height of competitive skill.

9. To defeat the competition by working very hard or to win by being lucky is no indication of great competitive skills.

10. Therefore, those who we will praise for being skilled in engaging the competition will first plan and create opportunities where the competition will lose before the competitive engagement begins.

11. For successful companies constantly strive to win without making mistakes. In their planning they do not tolerate useless activities, in their strategy there are no steps taken in vain.

12. A good manager takes up competitive positions in which he cannot lose and never misses an opportunity to defeat the competition.

13. Thus a successful company wins because it has managed the situations for victory before it occurs; a company destined for failure is so because they compete in the hope of winning with no planning. These companies are lead by people unable to accurately perceive their capabilities or understand how to act quickly and flexibly when faced with competition. These people engage the competition in a hesitant, stumbling manner without clear plans.

14. The good leader will be able to communicate his objectives clearly and will enforce discipline in the team that is engaging the competition.

15. This leader must be good in five skills.

16. First they must be good at qualifying potential customers or markets. This requires knowledge and insight into knowing when to compete and when not to compete.

17. Second they must be good at estimating costs, especially the cost of winning business or competing.

18. Third they must be good at analyzing strengths, both their own and the competition's.

19. Fourth, they must be good at calculating chances, forecasting the odds of winning against any competitor.

20. And fifth, they must be good at planning; especially the ability to successfully create winning plans against competitors, plans that are both good offensively and defensively.

21. It is because of the ability of leadership to understand and manage the disposition of their employees whether on the defense or offense, that a successful leader is able to make their people engage competition with such pent up emotions and energy that it has the effect of pent up flood

waters that when released burst forth with unstoppable force. Such a power can defeat any competitor.

Summary

As I stated in the beginning of this chapter, great competitive teams are not only good on offense but also great on defense. They know not only how to score when they have the ball but they are good at taking the ball away. It is not the height of sales or marketing skill to close business or own a market when you are already in control. What is the height of skill is to close when everything looks like the competition is going to win. This requires knowing the competition inside and out. You know how they think. You know what they are counting on to win. However, you are there before they are. You take away their winning tactics by anticipating them and creating a selling environment where those tactics will not only do not work but may, in fact, work against them.

Finally, Sun Tzu constantly brings up the importance of leadership. What does a leader need to now in order to lead, especially in sales and marketing? It is the responsibility of the leader to take the time to be educated about a number of things such as the strengths and weaknesses of the competition, how to qualify opportunities by understanding the markets you are competing in, planning a campaign, and estimating costs.

Chapter 5

Field Management

In some ways this may be the most important chapter. Sun Tzu understood the importance of leadership in winning a war. Like most of us in sales, I have had the chance to be a manager and to be managed. There is no substitute for good field leadership and management. Additionally, there is no bigger headache than poor field management. The skills to successfully lead and manage a field sales force are critical. It is important to understand how these skills are different than selling skills and how they affect the competitiveness of a company. Too often we promote the best tactician—a sales person or marketing person who was successful—without consideration of their leadership and management skills. Even worse, once we put a person in that position of leadership we do not train and develop them, leaving them to their own devices and hoping they will figure it out. Someone less obviously successful may be the better manager.

Remember Sun Tzu's traits of a good leader from an earlier chapter—wisdom, sincerity, humanity, courage, and discipline. Wisdom—they know what they are doing, they have been there and learned, and they are intelligent. They have not only been there but they learned the process and understand all the subtleness. Sincerity—they have a strong set of values and they practice them everyday, they believe or have "moral cause" in what the represent for the company. Humanity—they have empathy for their employees and customers, which tempers their judgment and makes people want to buy and work for them and give their best. Employees see them not only as managers but they see them as someone they can relate to. Courage—they can make the tough decisions and stand by them, they are not afraid to act. Discipline—they control themselves, they balance their lives, they do what they say they will do and expect this of others. They are very process driven so they understand not only the tactics of selling but also the whole process and strategy.

The field manager sets the tone for the direction that everyone else will follow. Also, a great manager will pay attention to the work environment and what are the values that are acted out. They set the culture for everyone and can as easily destroy a culture. This chapter is for field management.

Sun Tzu meant:
1. Generally, managing a large field sales force is the same as managing a small one. It is a matter how you divide or organize them.

2. And to control many people is the same as to control a few people. It is a matter of effective communication and discipline.

3. The ability to withstand a competitive engagement is due to the ability to understand the use of the direct (cheng) or indirect (ch'i) strategy. You must understand the use of direct confrontation and ambush of the competitor.

4. Always use your best ability against the competition's weakest.

5. Generally, in a competitive engagement use the direct confrontation to draw the competition in but use the surprise attack to win.

6. Those leaders who learn to be more indirect in their competitive approach will have an infinite variety of ways to surprise the competition and will not be limited in their approaches.

7. Although we talk of only two approaches, the direct and indirect (or frontal attack and ambush), their possible combinations provide an inexhaustible variety of possible competitive plans.

8. The leaders who understand this can create momentum that is overwhelming to the competition.

9. Also remember to strike the competition as swiftly as the falcon strikes its target. The reason the falcon breaks the back of its target is that the falcon awaits the right moment to strike. It is because of timing. The falcon regulates its movement thus the attack is precisely regulated and never falters because the falcon is sure it is time to strike.

10. Managers expert in engaging competition depend a lot on opportunity and expediency. They do not place the burden of winning on their employees alone.

11. In competing there are three kinds of advantages to try and create.

12. When, as a leader, you are not afraid of the competition and you have managers who love to take on the competition the morale will run high. This is an advantage in respect to morale.

13. When you have a market position that is a niche that is easy to defend like a narrow mountain pass, you can withstand the attack of a much larger competitor. This is advantage in respect to the market position.

14. When you can take advantage of the competition because they are lax or tired of competing and you can strike before they can get their market act together during their confusion, this is advantage in respect to the competition.

15. Therefore you must be able to recognize competitive situations that offer you great advantage because then it will take little effort on your part to create momentum that is unstoppable.

Summary

I have always believed and experienced that the key to any great sales force lies in the field management. It is certainly important to have great executive leadership. Likewise, it is important to attract and hire good people in the field. However, just like with a great army, it is the field commanders, sales management, which will determine true success or failure. If they have great morals, sincerity, intelligence, and discipline, you will have great execution. People will want to follow them and will follow their lead. If they are weak, the field sales force will be weak and turnover will be high. The manager must be good at setting the competitive mood for his reports. This person must be good at competing and helping the salespeople set competitive strategies. They should know every move of the competition in their area and be prepared to take them on. It should be an inspiration to work for and a leader.

I cannot tell you how many sales managers I know who were promoted because they were great sales people not necessarily great sales management material. These are two very different skill sets. They are related. I would never make someone a sales manager who had never sold. I am also always amazed at how little training most sales managers receive. That is most likely why great sales managers are not very common. However, I believe that if you look for the traits Sun Tzu points out and then give them training, you can have great field management.

Chapter 6

Strengths and Weaknesses

It is critical to understand what makes a sales force strong and what can weaken one. If you understand these things you can focus on strengthening your sales force and weakening the competition's. There are situations that will strengthen a sales force's chances of winning and those that are stages for disaster. It is important to recognize each. Strong sales forces are like tidal waves. They can crush those that oppose them, appearing suddenly and overwhelming the competition. Weak sales forces are easily confused and easily defeated. I have worked for both and it is a lot more fun and much more rewarding to work for a strong sales force. There is a sense of pride, of belonging to something special.

The strength of the sales force is independent of the product or service and independent of the individual's expertise. It is strong because of the environment management has created. The morale, the training, the belief in a common cause are all key.

Sun Tzu kind of said:

1. Generally, those who arrive first in the opportunity or market will be in a position to seize the initiative. Those who came late into the competition and have to rush into the competitive fray will be at a disadvantage. Note:

This is an important point for marketing. Always be on the look out for new or developing markets. It is easy to become complacent or comfortable in a market. It is like coming home to the same house everyday. Big or small, we know it and it is more comfortable. However, look at how drastically most markets have changed in the last 10 years or even the last 2 years!

There is a classic story of two companies. One defined itself as a buggy whip manufacturer the other as a transportation enhancer. One went out of business the other evolved into an automobile parts supplier. Marketing is the "look ahead" organization. How can we create a new market and then be the first to arrive and thrive? I will not beleaguer this point since there are mountains of books on marketing. However, I will recommend you make sure you have motivated, smart marketing people who are constantly thinking out of the marketing box you are currently in.

2. Therefore, those skilled in selling or marketing find or create the opportunity before the competition arrives rather than reacting to opportunities that have been created by the competition.

3. Use baits or false leads to get the competition to go where you want them to go. Hold strategic accounts to prevent the competition from making inroads where you do not want them.

4. To be able to confuse the competition is important to cause them to waste their resources.

5. Let the competition think you are in many places at once so they will have to spread out to meet you. This divides their attention and weakens their defense and offense.

6. Determine the competition's plans and strategies and keep yours hidden or difficult to uncover. This will allow you to know where to compete because you will know where the competitor will put their forces and you can concentrate you forces where the competitor is not or is weak.

7. With your effort concentrated on one opportunity and the competition's attention divided in 10 opportunities, the resources, which you use to attack, will be 10 times more powerful.

8. One who has fewer resources prepares against the competition, one who has many resources makes the competition prepare against them.

9. Thus Sun Tzu says that victory can be created. For even if the competition has greater resources, you can prevent them from being competitive if they do not know your strengths or weakness nor your strategies or plans. You can always cause them to think that they must urgently attend to their own preparations so that they do not have time to plan on how to compete effectively against you.

10. Therefore, determine the competitor's plans and strategies and you will know which plans and strategies will be successful and which will not.

11. Follow them and watch them to ascertain any patterns to how they do business.

12. Determine the competition's plans and how they like to compete and sell to ascertain what kind of customers they will go after.

13. Probe the competition and learn where they are strong and where they are weak.

14. For yourself it is important to not let the competition learn these things of you. When possible appear strong where you are weak and weak where you are strong. Do not appear to competition to have a plan or strategy. This will make it impossible for the competition to know how to plan against you.

15. Therefore, when I have won a victory, I do not repeat my tactics but respond to circumstances in a wide variety of ways.

16. You want to be as water, for just as moving water avoids high places and moves quickly to the low places, so you want to avoid the strengths of your competitors and attack their weaknesses.

17. And as the water's movement is according to the shape of the ground, so you must manage victory over you competition according to the situation of your customer, the market, and the competition.

18. Thus you will be able to gain victory by being able and willing to modify your tactics in accordance with the competitive situation.

Summary

This can be a difficult section since it talks a lot about doing things to confuse the competition. Our normal thinking is to just be better than the competition. We want to create better products and services. We want to have better sales people. We work to have better marketing. It is not necessarily normal to think about doing things to deceive the competition. Yet many athletic competitors will talk about psyching out the competition. How can they mess with their heads? Why would competition in business be any different? Certainly, we have seen this type of competing as we expand our global markets. I once worked for a company who had a particularly unethical competitor. Somehow one of this competitor's branch manager's was getting hold of the company's internal sales "top opportunities" list. While figuring out how to plug the leak (it ended up being the trash), they started issuing a false list and for several months saw very little of the competitor in the top opportunities.

This may sound a little over the edge, but there have been a number of articles on corporate espionage over the last ten years. It is real. I am not advocating it but I am saying if you are aware that it is being used, use that information to your advantage. As Sun Tzu says, find all matter of ways to deceive the enemy.

Sales teams are, by their nature, overly optimistic. This is good for morale but dangerous for competing. It is the job of sales management to honestly appraise the strengths and weaknesses of not only the sales team but also to appraise the strengths and weaknesses of all other competitive factors such as your position in the marketplace—what market or customers are you having success with and which ones are you not? Your products and services is another area—where do you add the most value to customers and where is it marginal? The best strategies in competing and war are those that constantly strive to play to your strengths. However, to do this you have to be brutally honest as management. Do not send your sales force off to compete like the charge of the "Light Brigade". Remember, while very brave, all in the charge of the light brigade died.

Chapter 7

Maneuvering Or Gaining an Advantageous Position

The market and competitors are ever changing. We are experiencing the fastest rate of change in history and it shows no signs of slowing down. Being able to quickly maneuver to either take advantage of change or avoid being crushed by it is of vital importance, especially with your field forces such as sales and marketing. Without the proper preparation for change you can become obsolete over night. In some industries the Internet is proving this. Understanding your position whether direct or indirect, and being able to maneuver the situation to your advantage is key. This is the realm of the strategist–to recognize the big picture, to see the players moving on the board. To understand what is going to happen and position yourself for victory is the height of competitive excitement. I have observed that one trait of a good strategist or analyst is to able to see patterns where others do not. However, you must be able to act on this knowledge and that is the art of maneuvering.

Sun Tzu might have said:
1. Nothing is more difficult than the art of maneuvering. What is difficult about maneuvering is to be able to make the quiet entry into the market and to turn competitive disadvantage into competitive advantage.
Note:
    I like this section because it introduces another dimension to marketing and selling—maneuvering. How well can you move your "pieces" on the market playing board to gain a competitive advantage? So many times I have seen corporate thinking that assumes almost everything is set and must be worked around. Our sales offices are in certain locations. We advertise in certain publications. We sell to certain markets. Be flexible! Think mobility! Move quickly to gain advantage!

2. A good strategy is getting to the customer or market first so as to gain an advantageous position with the customer against the competition.

3. A course of action, which may appear to put you at an advantage can also have the seeds of creating a disadvantage, so be cautious.

4. Remember, if you wait until you have everything you need to wage a competitive campaign you will move too slowly, if you engage the competition with no support you also risk being at a disadvantage and losing. It is a question of balance and timing.
Note:
    This piece is a reminder. For all that Sun Tzu talks about planning, he cautions us to balance it. You can plan too much. You can take to long to move. They key is to take enough time to understand what you are doing, get enough of the resources in place, and act! If you must move faster than

you can have everything in place, realize it and have contingencies. Do not let a quickly planned campaign become a poorly planned campaign. It is a question of balance and timing.

5. Those who do not understand their customer, the customer's environment, or the customer's market are not fit to lead their company into a competitive engagement.

6. Those who do not research the competitive arena ahead of time are unable to discern where their advantage can be and are also unfit to lead their company into a competitive engagement. Remember, it is offense AND defense.

7. In competing, one must be deceptive to the competitor and versatile to win.

8. Being able to take on the competition at the right moment, to maneuver your position with the customer or market effectively as the competitive situation changes is key.

9. He who knows the art of the direct and indirect approach will be successful. Such is the art of maneuvering.

10. When maneuvering against the competition it is important that your team have good communication and discipline. This is like an army who is disciplined and has good field communications.

11. If a company has been deprived of its morale, its executives will also lose heart. So be clear as to your purpose, your mission, and communicate it clearly to your people. Believe in what you are marketing!

12. During the start of a sales campaign the morale is high but as the campaign wears on the spirits can wan. Work to keep spirits high throughout the campaign.

13. And therefore those skilled in engaging the competition will avoid the competition when the competition's spirits are high and attack when their spirits become sluggish. This is control of the morale factor.

14. You should exercise discipline waiting for your competition to approach the customer in an undisciplined manner, be emotionally detached while your competitor becomes emotionally attached to the sale thus impairing their judgment.

15. Chose to compete in customers or markets that are close to your resources forcing the competition to support more remote engagements. This is control of the physical factor.

16. Those skilled in competitive engagements do not engage competitors who are better organized or who have much greater resources at the point of competition. This is control of the competitive circumstances.

17. Therefore, the art of maneuvering is that when the competition occupies the high ground (market or account domination) do not confront them. When the competitor cannot be surrounded or attacked indirectly, do not oppose them lightly.

18. Be careful of how the competition maneuvers for all may not be as it seems. As you plan to do to them so they may plan to do to you.

Summary

The tactics of maneuvering around the competition are important to understand. It is not enough to study and understand the competition if you do not act upon the information. You constantly hear in the business world today that an important trait is flexibility or market agility. This is maneuvering. Can you as a sales person maneuver yourself around the competition to win? Can you adapt to a changing competitive strategy? As a sales executive can you maneuver your resources quickly to adapt and win? As a marketing person, can you recognize the changing forces in the marketplace and adapt your marketing strategy and tactics? Can you move resources quickly to create or grab new markets?

Besides flexibility, information and communication are key to maneuvering. Do you have good information about the market or sales situation? Are you in constant communication with your team and management? As Sun Tzu pointed out, any good field commander understands that keeping the communications lines active during a battle is very important in order to first understand what is going on and, second, to be able to react quickly.

Chapter 8

The Nine Variables

It is important to study competitive selling in order to understand the principles that make competing successfully a process and not an event. When something is a process, the underlying principles that make it work are understood. Understanding these principles allows you to improve the process. It gives you control. Too often selling becomes a series of events that we are just reacting to. We do not understand that buying is a process of decision-making. This process can have several dimensions. Selling is also a process. As stated earlier, when you understand the entire situation and execute a strategy, you can begin to predict outcomes with more regularity. This is the essence of process—predictability. To work more efficiently and lower the typical stress of selling, you should be driven to make it a predictable process. You can only do this if you gain an understanding of what will drive it from the customer's perspective, your perspective, and the competitive perspective. To do this, study the variables and build guiding principles to help you understand the factors that are driving the process.

Sun Tzu implied:

1. Do not seek to establish market presence in customers that can easily be taken away by competition.

2. When competing for open territory, have strong partners.

3. Do not waste too much time winning accounts where there is little or no business just for the sake of owning the accounts. This is desolate ground.

4. In trying to win accounts or market where competitors surround you be clever about how you employ resources.

5. In desperate situations fight to the death.

6. There are some customers who are not worth pursuing.

7. There are some competitive situations not worth contesting.

8. There are some competitive installed bases you cannot win.

9. There are some competitors you may not be able to compete against.

10. When you see the right thing to do, act; do not wait for permission.

11. The leader must rely on their ability to control the situation to their advantage as opportunity dictates. They are not bound by established procedures.

12. The leader who does not understand the advantages of the nine variable competitive factors will not be able to use the customer situation to his advantage even though familiar with it.

13. The wise sales people always look at both the advantages and disadvantages when considering engaging the competition. Considering the advantages helps make any plan more feasible. Considering the disadvantages helps to prevent the plan from failing.

14. It is a doctrine of competitive engagements to prepare for the competition rather than hope they will not come. It is better to ensure your defensive posture rather than hope the competition will not attack.

15. There are five weaknesses that are dangerous in a sales or marketing manager.

16. If they are reckless and want to engage the competition without knowledge and planning they will lose.

17. If they are cowardly or afraid to compete they will not win.

18. If they are quick tempered they can be made a fool of by being provoked into competing without a sensible plan.

19. If they are too sensitive it is easy to insult or demoralize them so they won't compete.

20. If they are too emotional they become attached to an opportunity and will try to compete when they can no longer win.

21. These weaknesses cause poor judgment and make it impossible to create or execute strategy. They are the paths to failure for both the manager and the company.

Summary

Being driven by process is good. Being driven by events is bad. This fundamental principle applies to everything you do, not only competing. People driven by events do not understand the world around them. They simply react hoping they are doing the right thing. Every motivation speaker will tell you this. You can control a lot more than you think if you understand how to drive it to a process. Process comes with understanding and when you build those guiding principles that will keep you on track. Process can be improved. Events simply happen. When they are good events, we are happy. When they are bad events we are not. In either case, the fact that we see what happened as an event means we did not understand why it happened so it is very hard to either repeat or avoid.

My experience in life has been to observe that people who see life as a process or set of processes have lower stress and are happier. They feel in control. These people look to understand what are the guiding principles of any process that make a process work. Besides competing, look to understanding what goes on around you. Define your guiding principles. Understand and execute your processes. People driven by reacting to events feel out of control and things begin to break down. This is especially true of competing whether in selling or marketing.

Chapter 9

Mobilization

Mobilizing your forces so they are in a position to see the battle clearly is also important. Once the competitive battle starts, all the dust that is raised during the competitive battle can blur vision. There are reasons we constantly push the field to position themselves in an account or in a market as high as possible. The analogy is to get as far above the battle as possible so you can see beyond the "dust" of battle. As was stated earlier, we all feel that the pace of business is accelerating. This means that a key skill to competing is being able to quickly react and learn. It goes further than just being able to be in the right position though. Timing is important. Can you quickly mobilize your resources to be in the right place at the right time? Superior forces lost many battles because they could not mobilize quickly. So too it is with competing in business.

Sun Tzu meant:

1. Generally, when establishing your position in an account, call high up in the organization where you can get a clear, accurate view of the situation. The same is true of a market. When establishing your position, choose those customers who drive the market or "hold the high ground" as market leaders.

2. Engage the competition from a position high in the customer's organization. Do not try to start selling low in the organization and work your way up. Again the same is true of marketing. It is harder to build market presence that will create an advantageous market position from customers who are not seen as leading the market or who are seen as "holding the low ground".

3. This is important to remember when calling on companies that control decisions higher up.

4. When transitioning to new markets mobilize and do so quickly so the competition cannot take advantage of any distraction on your part.

5. When the competition is transitioning to new markets wait until they are in the middle of the transition to attack them. This leaves their resources divided yet committed between two or more markets and will slow their response.

6. Make sure you hold a higher position in the new market than the competition. This means more market share or more strategic customers.

7. When competing in soft markets, establish yourself in the strongest customers.

8. When competing in an open market be sure you know where the best accounts are and position yourself in an advantageous position with them so you have better access than the competition.

9. A competitive company prefers to call high rather than low and places a high value on competitive and customer knowledge. This keeps the sales organization healthy and helps them to occupy a firm position in the market. A sales force that does not suffer low morale and constant problems will be certain to be successful.

10. Look for signs of where the competition is and is going. These signs are important to recognizing what the competition's strategy may be.

11. When the sales people gather in small groups and whisper together, the management has lost their confidence.

12. Too frequent rewards indicate that management is at the end of their resources. Too frequent punishments indicate that management is in acute distress.

13. If management treats the employees poorly and later is in fear of them, the limit of discipline has been reached.

14. When the competitor is in high spirits but will not compete nor leave the market, you must investigate this situation.

15. In competing, size alone does not confer advantage. Do not compete relying on sheer size.

16. It is sufficient to correctly estimate the competitor and competitive situation and concentrate your effort where your strength is to win. It could not be stated more simply. The person who does not plan or have a competitive strategy and underestimates the competition will lose.

17. Finally, the management must take care in how they manage the sales force in order to build and maintain loyalty. If they manage them with civility and fairness and imbue them uniformly with competitive spirit they will be successful.

Summary

When you think of mobilization think about all it takes to get an army in place to do battle. Now think about how much planning and effort it takes to change that army's position. All resources have to be re-positioned. Now try to understand why, when as a sales person you run into the boss's office and declare there is an important competitive battle you are engaged in and you need resources now, the boss looks at you annoyed. The issue is, if you knew there was a battle and you were going to need resources, why did you wait until it became critical to ask for them? This is bad planning and very tactical.

You get frustrated when the manager says, "The resources you need are not available right now. If, several weeks ago, I had known you would need them today, we could have planned for it". In interviewing sales managers, one of their top pet peeves was crisis management of resources caused by sales people running in and demanding resources at the last moment. It is hard to mobilize resources at the spur of the moment. I applaud companies who are so agile they can do it but I guarantee they cannot do it every time. No one has unlimited resources.

Chapter 10

Markets and Customers

Before deciding to enter a market, it is important to stand back and analyze the characteristics of that market in order to make a strategic decision as to whether or not to enter it and if you are going to enter what should you expect. Today's markets are in vast change with new players, new customers, new technologies, new competitive rules, and new business models. If you are a computer manufacturer, how could you have predicted Dell's introduction of a completely new business model for selling and marketing? Not one computer company at the time saw it coming or believed it would work. By the time they realized their mistake it was too late. Dell has such a lead it is questionable if anyone can catch up and even who will survive. It will pay to have someone who is able to stand back and see the whole picture in order to assist in your strategy and in position your company to win. Using this knowledge you can classify markets according to some common behaviors.

Sun Tzu kind of said:

1. Markets and customers may be classified according to how accessible they are: easy, entrapping, neutral, niche, dangerous, and distant.

2. Markets and customers that are accessible to both you and competition are called easy. The company or person who gets here first and establishes a presence in the right accounts or in an account with the right people will have an edge over the competition. You must also have your resources accessible to this market.

3. Markets that are easy to enter but difficult to withdraw from are called entrapping. It is easy to engage the competition when they are unprepared in this type of market, but it is difficult if they are well prepared and, yet, it may be impossible to withdraw from this type of market. This type of customer or market may be unprofitable over time.

4. Markets or accounts that are equally difficult or impossible for you and the competition to enter are neutral. You must never be tempted into trying to win this type of market or account. Let the competition waste their resources trying.

5. In a niche market, you should try to be the first to establish yourself and wait for the competition to try and compete. If the competition is first in the niche market you should not try to follow them unless they have not been able to effectively establish themselves.

6. These are accounts or markets where, because of your resources or capabilities, you are most vulnerable. In this situation you must be the first to occupy the high ground or accounts and establish relationships with people

who give you the upper hand in the account or market. If the competition holds the high ground first, do not try to compete with them. It will probably be fatal.

7. When you and the competition occupy accounts that are not closely related either by distance or type of market it will probably be difficult to compete and unprofitable to engage them in competing for accounts they already hold.

8. These are principles of six different types of markets or accounts. It is important that you understand these and how they can help or prevent success.

9. There are six disasters in competing that can be attributed to poor management. These are when field sales forces flee from competition, are insubordinate, are demoralized, collapse in disorder, or are thoroughly beaten.

10. When a force one tenth the size of a competitor is ordered to compete, the result is a fear of competition and inability to compete.

11. When the sales force is strong but the management is weak the sales force will be insubordinate.

12. When the sales management is aggressive but the sales people are ineffective, the sales people will be demoralized.

13. When the executives are morally weak and their discipline is not strict, when their instructions and guidance are not clear and visionary, when there are no consistent values to guide field managers and sales people, the sales force will be in disorder.

14. When a field sales manager is unable to estimate the competition's strength and underestimates the resources needed, the result is a thorough defeat.

15. Managers must be held responsible for these causes of defeat. The causes of defeat must be carefully studied and understood in order to be avoided.

16. Understanding the customer or market situation can help to put your sales force in an advantageous position but it is superior leadership that puts the advantage to good use.

17. You should engage the competition only when you are sure of winning. When you are sure of defeat but management has ordered you to compete you should ignore the manager's orders, if you can, and not engage the competition.

18. A good sales leader does not engage the competition to seek personal glory nor do they order the sales force to retreat from competing in order for the leader to avoid personal disgrace. Their purpose is to help make their employees and their company successful. This type of sales or marketing leader is very valuable.

19. Such a leader treats his employees well with compassion, concern, humanity, and discipline. The employees will return this type of leadership with undying loyalty.

20. However, be cautioned. If a leader indulges his employees but is unable to cause them to work, or obey his directions, or to be disciplined in their work, and therefore they are out of control, these employees are compared to spoiled children and are useless.

23. If, as a sales leader, I know that my sales people are capable of taking on the competition, but I am unable to discern that in a given situation

the competition is invulnerable, my chance of winning is but half. The reverse is also true.

24. So it is said, "Know the competition and know yourself; your victory will never be in peril. If you also know the customer, and know the market, your victory will be total.

Summary

This chapter is mainly for sales and marketing management. This chapter deals with the big picture. Are you able to understand the different types of markets and customers? They are there. They have discernable characteristics. Understanding them allows you to recognize them and make more strategic decisions relative to deploying your sales force to compete in them. This type of decision-making has all kinds of ramifications. Better use of resources and higher employee morale are just two.

Take time to rise above the everyday minutiae to gain insight into your territory or markets. Understand their behavior and you will see clearer paths on how to effectively compete. Are you an industry expert in the industries you compete in and the markets you sell to? As a manager, you should be. Are you a student of the competitors that your field people face everyday. As a leader, you should be. Leadership is such an important topic. There are many books and courses on leadership and this one adds a few insights to this important topic. As sales or marketing manager, please pay attention to them.

Chapter 11

The Nine Classic Situations

In warfare and competing there are rarely new situations. The combination of competitors, customer ground, markets, and strategic thinking combine time and time again to create common situations. I once read "Those who are unwilling to study the past and learn from it will be destined to repeat it. The past is but a prologue to the future". Again, this is why in chess you see that the masters know every possible strategy and how it plays out. They may think of slight variations, usually to confuse the opponent, but the basic moves are the same. The same occurs in competing. I understand that there are new business models being created everyday but as one executive friend of mine in high tech sales said recently, "The basics to competing still apply if you truly understand them".

There may be variations or new combinations but the basic situations are usually the same. It is this ability to instantly recognize the patterns and be able to know exactly how to react in order to gain the upper hand. Humans are shown in study after study to be creatures of habit. We like some repetition. New models may be formed but even they will settle down to patterns after the initial experimentation. These situations are related to your competitive positioning in your territory or market. Recognize what situation you are in and it will direct your strategy. After all, in the history of warfare a lot has changed but Sun Tzu is still studied in most war colleges today after 2300 years so a lot has stayed the same.

Sun Tzu might have said:
1. In the market or customer environment there are nine classifications: dispersive, frontier, key, open, commanding, serious, difficult, dangerous, and desperate.

2. When defending an installed base you are in dispersive territory.

3. When you are just penetrating the competition's installed base it is frontier territory.

4. Territory that is equally advantageous to defend for you or the competition is key or strategic territory. This ground will be easy for the first to occupy to defend against competitive intrusion.

5. When territory is not occupied by you or competition but is equally accessible by both it is open territory.

6. When you control a strategic part of the market you have commanding territory.

7. When someone has committed serious resources to a market and won apiece that is surrounded by the competition it is in serious territory.

8. When you are faced with entering a market that is not easy to enter, compete in, or win it is difficult territory.

9. Territory that can only be won if you "bet your company", which means that if you don't win you go out of business, is called desperate territory.

10. And therefore, protect dispersive territory by not allowing competition to even begin to compete in it; when possible, pass by frontier territory.

11. Do not attack a competitor who occupies key or strategic territory; in open territory keep your resources focused so they will not get distracted.

12. In commanding territory take advantage of your position to expand.

13. In serious territory, be careful to use your resources wisely.

14. In difficult territory pass through quickly.

15. In desperate territory compete like you never have before.

16. In the far past, those described as skilled in defeating the competition, made it impossible for the competition to unite their forces because of the strategies employed. These strategies kept the competition unaware of where they would engage and so threw them into confusion.

17. Those skilled at engaging the competition concentrated their resources and competed when it was advantageous to do so. When it was not advantageous to compete they did not.

18. Should you ask how to deal with a well disciplined competitive sales force I would reply by telling you to seize an account they cherish and you will demoralize them.

19. Speed is the essence of competitive selling or marketing. Take advantage of the competition's unprepared ness. Remember that the beginning of competitive advantage begins with one piece of important customer information one day earlier than the competition.

20. Approach the market and customers from unexpected ways and strike the competition where they have not protected themselves.

21. A general principle of an invading sales force is that when you have been successful at taking accounts or market share away from the competition, your people will be united in their morale and it will be harder for the competition to beat you.

22. When you have uncovered an open account or market that is fertile for your product or service, sell as much as you can as fast as you can to provide financial resources for yourself that you will need later. Do not take your time.

23. Pay heed to the financial and emotional needs of your employees. Do not overwork and underpay them. Unite them in spirit; conserve their energy.

24. Those managers who are not familiar with the advantages and pitfalls of the market place cannot lead the sales force into competition.

25. Those who are unable to establish important alliances in the market place will find it difficult to gain a lead.

26. Those who are unable to determine who in the customer can best guide them in an account or market will not be able to understand the customer situations and gain a political advantage.

27. Lacking in any of these three areas is poor marketing or managing.

28. To ensure that the sales force can compete as a unified force, the management must maximize the strength of each of his salespeople, both the weak and the strong. Also the manager has to know how to gain from the market conditions.

29. It is the business of the top executive to be serene so he may not be vexed, to be inscrutable so competition will not be able to know what he thinks, to be impartial so as to be seen as fair and able to identify the best for the job, and self-controlled so as not to become confused.

30. The best sales or marketing management must be able to change their methods of competing and alter the plans so the competition has no knowledge of what they are doing. This makes it impossible for the competition to anticipate their purpose.

31. When the competition is ignorant of your plans they cannot easily prepare plans to defeat you: when they are ignorant of the conditions driving and determining the market they cannot properly disperse their sales force; if the competition fails to identify and use insiders to the market or customer they cannot gain an advantage over you. An executive ignorant of even one of these three matters is unfit to lead a sales force but makes for a fun competitor that can be easily beaten.

32. A manager or salesperson worthy of the title "Strategist" is so because he can defeat the competition without directly competing by anticipating the competition's plans. This is known as ability to win with ease.

33. When the competition presents an opportunity for you to win, be in a position to immediately take advantage of it. Know your competition well enough to understand what customers or markets he values. Anticipate this and seize what he values in secret so as not to alert him.

34. In the beginning behave like an inexperienced sales or marketing person in order to seduce the competition into complacency then spring a surprise attack as swift as a hare in order to catch the competition off guard.

Summary

Remember we said in the beginning of this book that one of the key questions for any sales person or manager is "How can I dominate my territory?" It starts with an assessment of your position in the territory. How many possible targets are there in my territory or market? How many of those targets do I currently "own"? Which are strongholds of my competition? Which accounts are "head dominos" that if I win will cause other victories? What can I win this year, quarter, or month? Which should I target for later? Once you can honestly assess your current position you will know your next move, your strategy for the foreseeable future.

In competing, as was said at the start of this chapter, there will emerge patterns or "classic situations". Understanding these and recognizing them when they occur will allow you to react more quickly, plan ahead, and be moves ahead of your competition. How much more fun could that be? To repeat an earlier analogy, this is the game of chess. To be able to recognize the playing pattern of your foe and anticipate how they will play the game is the art of the strategist. People behave in patterns. Look for them. Anticipate them. Plan to defeat them.

Chapter 12

Disrupting the Competition

It is not enough to know the competition. You must have tactics to defeat them. You need to know what they are counting on to win and remove it from the equation. It does begin with knowing the competition, understanding their strategy, knowing their strengths and weaknesses. Once this knowledge is gained, however, it is time to put in place plans to defeat them, to cause them to fail. This is more tactical and follows determination of your strategy. Look at all the great military leaders and you will see someone who understands the enemy. Sometimes they understand them better than the enemy understands themselves. Understanding them allows you to understand how to disrupt their plans but you must also be prepared to take action.

As Sun Tzu points out, there are many ways to disrupt the plans of the competition. It starts with understanding what they are counting on to win. Other considerations are things such as the training and support they give the sales force. Usually, by the time you are able to determine these things, the competition is totally committed to them. This is why being able to disrupt their plans is important. This causes confusion and can be hard for a competitor to recover from. A large company I once worked for found itself with a big problem. Their primary competitor was hiring away their best people with great ease. What they later learned was that the competitor had learned of their sales compensation plan, which was not very good at the high end, and used the fact to lure away the best sales people. By the time the company realized this fact, they had lost most of their top people. It could be called unfair but it was very disrupting and could have been prevented.

Sun Tzu might have said:
1. There are five methods to disrupt the competition. The first is to hire away the best people, the second is to cause them to waste their resources, the third is make their marketing impotent, the fourth is to make their sales strategies useless, the fifth is to disrupt their workforce.
Note:
As I have pointed out earlier, the idea of actually implementing tactics to disrupt the competition may be uncomfortable to some. However, when put into these categories, most of it makes sense. As I talked about in the introduction, it is very common for one competitor to hire away another's top people. It is certainly not uncommon for a company to work at undermining another's marketing efforts or sales strategies. What is more interesting is the concept of finding ways to cause the competition to waste resources or disrupt their workforce.

2. In order to disrupt the enemy you need good intelligence on them, preferably some inside information.

3. A group of competitive specialists must always be on hand so as to be able to exploit a situation. You should prepare ahead of time to be able to exploit any situation.

4. The conditions must be right and you must be prepared before attempting to disrupt the competition.

5. There are certain conditions that are more favorable than others to disrupting the competition. You must study and be aware of what these conditions are.

6. When you are employing tactics to disrupt, be in a position to react to changing conditions to effect the maximum disruption.

7. When disruption or confusion occurs in the competition's camp, immediately coordinate your reaction. But if his employees remain calm and do not react, bide your time and do not execute your plan.

8. When the disruption reaches its height, follow up with your counter move if you can. If, for whatever reason, you cannot execute a counter move simply wait for the disruption to play itself out.

9. If you can cause disruptions from outside the competitor's environment do not wait until you have the ability to cause it from within the competitor's environment. Cause disruptions whenever you can but do not let the disruption cause disruption in your environment.

10. When you openly take on your competitor do not do so in the direction of the disruption you have caused. This will help keep you from also being disrupted and will cause further disruption to the competition

because they will feel like they are being attacked from several directions at once.

11. Remember that disruptions are best fed during working hours when the competitor's internal cultural networks will "fan the flames".

12. Now the sales force must know the five ways to disrupt and be constantly vigilant so they are not used against you.

13. Those who use disruptions as part of their sales campaigns are being very smart. Those who can use all they have to overwhelm their competition are marketing powerhouses.

14. There are conditions of the marketplace that can limit a competitor's ability to compete but few that can cause him to waste resources or ruin his strategies.

15. To win competitive battles and accomplish your objectives but fail to truly exploit these situations is a lost opportunity that may come back to haunt you later.

16. Compete only to win. Don't openly move against a competitor if there is nothing of value to gain.

17. Don't ask salespeople to compete if winning is impossible and don't openly declare war on the competition unless the situation is desperate. Note:
     As history has shown, declaring open war on another is a recipe for disaster and should be a last resort. It is much better to go by more circuitous routes. We all know we are competing. However, it raises the emotions of your competitors when you openly declare war. You should always strive to be subtle. This way you may be able to win the war without the competitor realizing there really was one. Also, remember, it is also demoralizing to be asked to fight a battle you know you cannot win, especially for a sales person.

18. Leaders must not declare war on a competitor in anger. Field managers must not compete out of spite. Only go to war on a competitor when the company and the customer have some definite gains. An angry leader can become happy but a company that is driven to bankruptcy out of sheer madness cannot be restored.

Note:

This is another important point about management. There seems to be this idea that managers should be up in front, yelling and screaming, in order to be leaders. The truth is that we need dispassionate leaders. We need leaders who care and believe in what they are doing but can go about it in a levelheaded fashion. Too often I have seen executives or sales managers who become so emotional about going after an account that all good judgment goes out the window. As Sun Tzu points out, this is a dangerous competitive situation. If I were the more objective competitor in that situation, I would fan your flame of emotion in order to cloud your judgment and get you to say or do something that would cause the customer to not want to do business with you.

19. Enlightened leaders spend much time creating plans and good managers execute them.

20. A wise leader will consider all matters relating to competing carefully because the concern the thriving or bankruptcy of the company.

Summary

The concepts in this chapter can be uncomfortable for some people. In western culture especially we have this overriding sense of "fair play". Is it fair to employ tactics that disrupts the competition? This can be a tough question. How badly do you want to win? How confident are you that your competition will not only try to disrupt you, but also your markets, or your customers? It is my experience that in today's world, the competition is willing to disrupt me to win the business. How much attention you are willing to devote to this idea will depend on many factors, not the least of which is what type of competitor are you? There are tactics that are perfectly ethical but very disruptive by most rules.

In the next chapter, we will explore how you gather the information to accomplish what we discussed in this chapter. As you can see, the theme over and over in Sun Tzu's writings on competing, on defeating the competition is knowing your competition so you will know what strategies and tactics will work and which ones will not. You must know the competition, and be willing to act.

Chapter 13

Gathering Intelligence

Probably the hardest topic to discuss in western corporate culture is that of "gathering intelligence" or spying. No intelligent general in the history of warfare would have considered going into battle without as much intelligence on the enemy as possible. In business we deal with our different cultural ethics regarding "spying" or gathering intelligence on our competition and indeed there is a line in almost any culture that can be crossed that should not be crossed. When these lines are crossed, laws are now broken and, if caught, people will be punished. I'm not talking about that level but rather the level of intelligence gathering that many times can be accomplished by simply being very observant.

There is a lot of competitive information just lying around waiting for someone to really see it and analyze it. Analyze a competitor's advertising to understand how they are positioning themselves. What markets are they targeting? What do their brochures emphasize? Analyze their sales forces and selling patterns to understand how they will behave in the customer or in a particular market. How do they present their products or services to prospects? Where do they enter an account? Analyzing their management methods. How are they deploying their field force? Analyze their senior management. What does their annual report say about strategic issues? The best sales organization I ever worked for had a department dedicated to gathering and analyzing competitive information. They then disseminated this to the sales force in the form of how to beat the competition. Without mentioning the company's name, they were almost always number one in their industries without superior products.

Every company should have a person dedicated to knowing the competition, gather information from the field and other sources. Many companies will say they do this but they do not, at least not very well. Finally, it is the responsibility of each field sales person to do their own intelligence gathering. How is the competition behaving in my territory? Do I know who they are? How do they sell? What do they count on to win? What might that tell me about how to defeat them? Where are they vulnerable? Good competitive intelligence is the most important factor in preparing to compete. Also, you need intelligent people who can analyze the intelligence and help prepare plans to act on the information.

Sun Tzu meant:
1. It costs both the employees and the company a lot of money every day to establish and maintain a strong sales force. The costs can be as much as seven times the cost per other types of employees.

2. Sales forces have to put in a lot of effort and use precious resources in order to get in a position to win. A leader or executive who does not

understand the importance of gathering competitive information, thus resulting in his losing the sale, is not worthy to be a leader, is no support to his company, and can not be a master of victory.

3. Wise leaders and capable managers win because they have knowledge of the competition's strategies, tactics, strengths, and weaknesses.

4. This information cannot be obtained through astrology, ouji boards, or through conjecture. This information can only be obtained from people who have a thorough knowledge of the competitor's situation.

5. There are five types of people who can give or get information. These are customers, insiders, hires, market researchers, and consultants.

6. These sources of competitive information can work wonders when they are put to good use and they are valuable assets to any company.

7. Customers are those customers of the competition who are willing to share their experiences with you. These people can give information that shows what the competitor does in actual practice.
Note:
    One of the more clever ways of gathering this type of information that I have seen is to employ an outside research firm to research customers in your industry to understand buying and selling practices. This can be done as pure research and you can get a wealth of information.

8. Insiders are people who work for the competition and are willing to share information knowingly or unknowingly with you.
Note:
    It is amazing what people will spill in casual conversation. This is especially true if your whole organization is attuned to gathering competitive information. In one industry I have sold in there was a particularly aggressive competitor who was very good at engaging competitive sales and marketing

people in casual conversation at trade shows and conferences. Just listening in on a few conversations, I was amazed at what was spilled with a few well-placed questions.

9. Hires are those people that you hire away from the competition and can be debriefed for valuable information. These people may also be able to supply insiders.

10. Market researchers can provide information that extends over time and is comparative in nature. Their information can be limited, especially if they have agreements with the competition.

11. Consultants can provide another view of the information, especially if they have done extensive work for the competition. Like market researchers, be careful! While pretending to be independent, many times these people also have relationships with competition.

12. Of all those within your company, none should be as close to executives as those who supply competitive information; of all rewards none more liberal than those given to these people; of all matters none are more confidential than these.
Note:
   I do need to make this note here. Many times these people who gather and analyze competitive information are kept away from executive management. Their information gets filtered so that by the time it reached the ears of people who can take strategic action, it does not resemble the original research. This is many times because of inside politics. I have seen this "shoot the messenger" fear in many companies. I have seen many executives who do not want to hear anything negative, fearing it is like a virus that can spread. Wise executives will not let this happen. If you are a sales or marketing executive, talk directly to these people. Listen to what they have to say unfiltered. Hear the truth of any situation. Only then can you act correctly.

13. Only the very clever leaders can put competitive intelligence to good use. Only the generous and humane can obtain any information they wish from these "spies". Only the very cautious and ingenious can tell whether the intelligence reports are accurate.

Note:

All competitive intelligence is suspect. This is why people of special intelligence should analyze it. Earlier I mentioned that it takes a special talent to truly analyze competitive information. These people must be able to look for patterns. They must be able to sift through the information and understand what is true and what is not or what is good and what is bad information.

14. It is a delicate matter but intelligence can and should be used anywhere. Remember, "Business is war".

15. If these "informants" are not careful in what they say or to whom, they should not be used anymore.

16. Before calling on a prospect or taking on a competitor, first find out who their leaders are and whom the leaders rely on. You must use your intelligence network to gather this information in minute detail.

17. Find out whom the competition is using inside the customer and try to win them over so you can feed false information to the competition.

18. If you wish to be able to take on the competition effectively, you must know the people employed by the competition. Are they smart or stupid, clever or clumsy?

19. Wise leaders and brilliant managers will be able to spot good talent for competitive information and will be successful in recruiting them.

20. Gathering intelligence is the most important work in competing because there can be no competitive plans without good information about the competition.

Summary

As I stated at the start of this chapter, this is the most delicate discussion to have in a business but it is also one of the most important. To compete with little, inaccurate, or no competitive information is to almost ensure failure. Again, no general would even think of engaging the enemy without some form of intelligence. How many times in recent years have we criticized governments in times of crisis for their lack of good intelligence about an adversary? Many famous battles have turned on the information gained beforehand about the enemy. Many battles have been lost due to missing or bad competitive information.

The key is that there are usually plenty of chances to gather competitive information without resorting to unethical means such as going through competitor's trash, even though this is not necessarily illegal and in some countries is even common practice. The key is to make the gathering of intelligence a common practice in a company. It should be part of the marketing process. Simple observation and analysis can go a long way to help you understand a competitor's mindset. Do you know your competition as well as they know themselves? If not, you are at a competitive disadvantage. It is hard to predict a competitor's moves if you have not studied them. In this mode of little or no good intelligence, you compete in the hope that you are better.

Epilogue

This concludes this sales and marketing orientation to the "Art of War". Some of the concepts may seem harsh but I believe that most of us realize that as the world of business becomes increasingly more global, the rules of competing become increasingly more complex and quite frankly, more ruthless. All of these concepts can be applied in the context of a particular society's ethics, which we know vary widely around the world. The key is to be able to compete so as to not only survive but to thrive. Remember Sun Tzu' opening words; "Competing is a matter of vital importance to the company; the province of profit or loss; the road to survival or ruin. It is mandatory that it be thoroughly studied".

I have found that my journey to sales and marketing has been very rewarding. As I said in the beginning of this book, it was not a journey I anticipated. It just happened. I hope more and more schools take up the banner of helping make sales a legitimate profession. I do not believe that the great sales people are just born. I believe they become great while traveling down a tough road and learning a lot of lessons. Great sales and marketing people learn and then apply their lessons. At the heart of a great sales or marketing person is a very competitive person.

Being able to compete well should be the goal of not only the sales department but of the entire company. This is especially true of management. There has to be a commitment to doing it well from the top down. Some resources will need to be committed to tracking and analyzing the competition. You need to be able to get into the heads of your competitors and understand what makes them tick and how they will react under a variety of circumstances. Being able to out-think the competition should be the goal of both the marketing team and the sales team. Know where they are going to walk and put obstacles in their path to cause them to stumble.

Last, if I can point you to any key area it would be Sun Tzu's observations on leadership. For field people this is critical. As Sun Tzu points out, if the field leadership is weak, you are doomed. If your top leadership is weak or lacking in conviction, you are doomed. There is no way to word-smith our way around these facts.

I hope this translation will help you understand Sun Tzu's concepts. As I said in the beginning of this book, these concepts are as applicable today as they were 3000 years ago. They are especially applicable to sales and marketing people. Now go out and beat the competition!

About the Author

Scott Bell is currently a marketing executive with EDS in their PLM Solutions line of business. He has a degree in Architecture from the University of Illinois and an MBA from the University of Missouri. Scott has been in field sales, sales management, marketing, strategic planning, and sales training for 25 years. Scott has been certified in a number of different sales training courses as an instructor along with attending a number of other sales courses. Scott has conducted sales training in Europe and Asia as well as the Americas. During Scott's career he sold for IBM's Office Products Division, McDonnell Douglas Automation, Unigraphics Solutions, Graphic Data Solutions, and EDS. Scott's sales roles included field salesperson, sales manager, National Account Sales Manager, Director–National Sales, and Vice President of Global Sales Programs. Scott has also held positions in product marketing, strategic planning, and run global sales programs such as global sales meeting and sales incentive award trips. Finally, Scott has been a speaker at the annual National Account Manager's Association (NAMA) meeting.

Scott is on the Missouri Advisory Board for the International Business Internship Exchange and will participate as a mentor in the St. Louis University MBA Program in the spring of 2002.

0-595-21488-6